GW00383907

DO YOU KNOW THEM?

Endangered Animals Book Grade 4 |
Children's Nature Books

BABY PROFESSOR
EDUCATION KIDS

First Edition, 2020

Published in the United States by Speedy Publishing LLC, 40 E Main Street, Newark, Delaware 19711 USA.

© 2020 Baby Professor Books, an imprint of Speedy Publishing LLC

Baby Professor Books are available at special discounts when purchased in bulk for industrial and sales-promotional use. For details contact our Special Sales Team at Speedy Publishing LLC, 40 E Main Street, Newark, Delaware 19711 USA. Telephone (888) 248-4521 Fax: (210) 519-4043.

10 9 8 7 6 * 5 4 3 2 1

Print Edition: 9781541953482
Digital Edition: 9781541956483
Hardcover Edition: 9781541977044

See the world in pictures. Build your knowledge in style.
www.speedypublishing.com

CONTENTS

You may read about endangered animals or hear about them on television, but do you know what that really means? You know about dinosaurs and how they once roamed the Earth millions of years ago before they eventually died out. It is sad to think about, but that happens to a lot of animals. They develop into a species, thrive on Earth for a long time, and then the whole species dies out. It is still happening today. Some of our favorite animals of today may not be around when your grandchildren are born. In this book, we will take a quick look at how scientists classify endangered animals, some of the reasons why animals become endangered, and what we can do to help them. Lastly, we will look at some of the most endangered animals on the planet today. Let's get started.

THE CONSERVATION STATUS OF ANIMALS

Some animals are in danger of becoming extinct[1] very soon while others are thriving. Scientists have developed a ranking system to know which animals are more threatened than others. There are actually several different ranking systems in use, but the most commonly used one is the Red List of Threatened Species that is compiled by the IUCN, or International Union for Conservation of Nature.

Logo for the IUCN Red List.

[1] Extinct – No longer in existence

Animals are categorized into one of nine different categories on the Red List of Threatened Species based on the size of their population, growth rate, and size of habitat.

THE RED LIST CATEGORIES

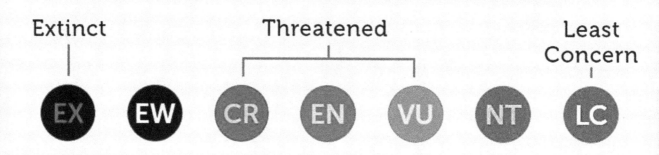

Extinct

Threatened

Least Concern

EX EW CR EN VU NT LC

Extinct (EX): no reasonable doubt that the last individual has died

Extinct in the Wild (EW): known only to survive in captivity, cultivation or well outside its natural range

Critically Endangered (CR): facing extremely high risk of extinction in the wild

Endangered (EN): facing a very high risk of extinction in the wild,

Vulnerable (VU): facing a high risk of extinction in the wild.

Near Threatened (NT): close to qualifying, or likely to qualify for a threatened category in the near future

Least Concern (LC): population is stable enough that it is unlikely to face extinction in the near future

Data Deficient (DD): not enough information on abundance or distribution to estimate its risk of extinction

The categories include extinct and extinct in the wild animals. After that, the most alarming categories are critically endangered and endangered, followed by vulnerable[2] and near threatened. Animals of least concern are followed by two more categories, data deficient and not evaluated, for animal species that have not yet been assessed for extinction risk.

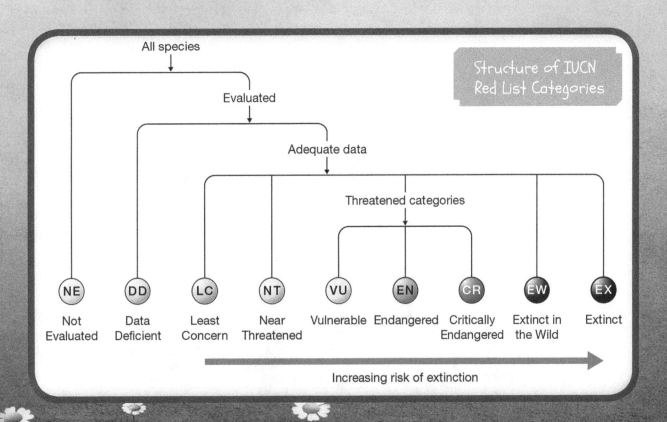

Structure of IUCN Red List Categories

All species

Evaluated

Adequate data

Threatened categories

NE	DD	LC	NT	VU	EN	CR	EW	EX
Not Evaluated	Data Deficient	Least Concern	Near Threatened	Vulnerable	Endangered	Critically Endangered	Extinct in the Wild	Extinct

Increasing risk of extinction

[2] Vulnerable – In a position to be hurt or damaged

WHY DO ANIMALS BECOME ENDANGERED?

An animal species becomes threatened with extinction in one of two ways...through the loss of their habitat or due to declining genetic diversity. It may sound rather simple to say that there are only two ways that an animal species becomes extinct, but each one of these is more complex than you may think. There are several different causes that contribute to each of these factors. In the next two sections, we will look at habitat loss and declining genetic diversity more closely.

LACK OF FOOD

CAUSES OF EXTINCTION

ASTEROID STRIKE

CLIMATE CHANGE

BETTER-ADAPTED COMPETITION

INVASIVE SPECIES

DISEASE

LACK OF GENETIC DIVERSITY

HUMAN PREDATION

HABITAT LOSS

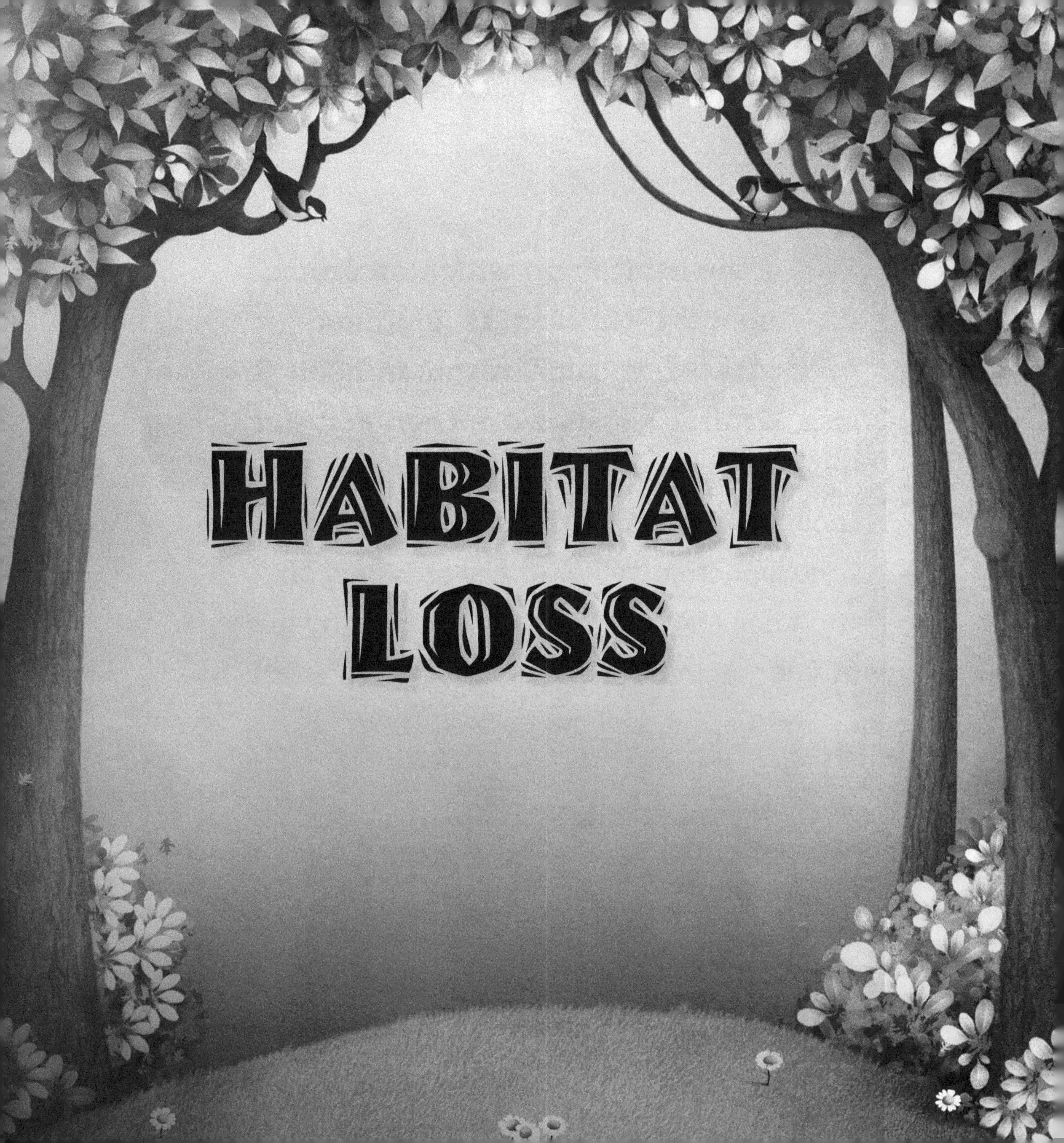

If the habitat[3] in which an animal species thrives is changed or altered, it could result in habitat loss. Habitat loss is more than just not having enough space to live. It also includes changes to the habitat that make it no longer suitable for the animals. This includes the loss of trees or other forms of vegetation, temperature, and rainfall changes, and decline in food sources.

[3] Habitat – The natural environment of a living thing

Habitat loss includes the loss of trees or other forms of vegetation.

Clearing of land for housing development in Charlotte, North Carolina

Habitat loss can happen through natural events or through human activity. Planting large farm fields, clearing trees to make room for housing developments, and industries that contribute to global warming are all factors in habitat loss.

Genetic **diversity**[4] refers to the number of different genes spread out throughout the animals in the species.

[4] Diversity – Having differences and variety

24

The diversity that an animal has in its gene pool better equips the whole species in adapting to changes in habitat.

Dogs of different breeds

When the population of a species becomes too small, inbreeding occurs and the diversity of the species declines. Inbreeding can lead to severe health issues, less resistance to disease, and reproductive problems, which further depletes the population.

Low genetic diversity and resulting poor sperm quality has made breeding and survivorship difficult for cheetahs.

Two camouflaged waterfowl hunters during duck hunting

When humans overhunt or overfish a habitat, the numbers of animals decline to the point where genetic[5] diversity is lost. Declining genetic diversity can also occur naturally.

[5] Genetic – Pertaining to the genes in a living thing

DO YOU KNOW THESE ENDANGERED ANIMALS?

Unfortunately, there are several animals currently listed as endangered or critically endangered on the Red List of Threatened Species. The populations of these animals are dwindling in the wild, despite conservation efforts by biologists and scientists. Some of these animals are well-known, but others may not be. All of these animal species are important. They contribute to their ecosystem in one way or another so their loss will have an impact. The following sections look at ten different endangered species that are currently on the Red List of Threatened Species.

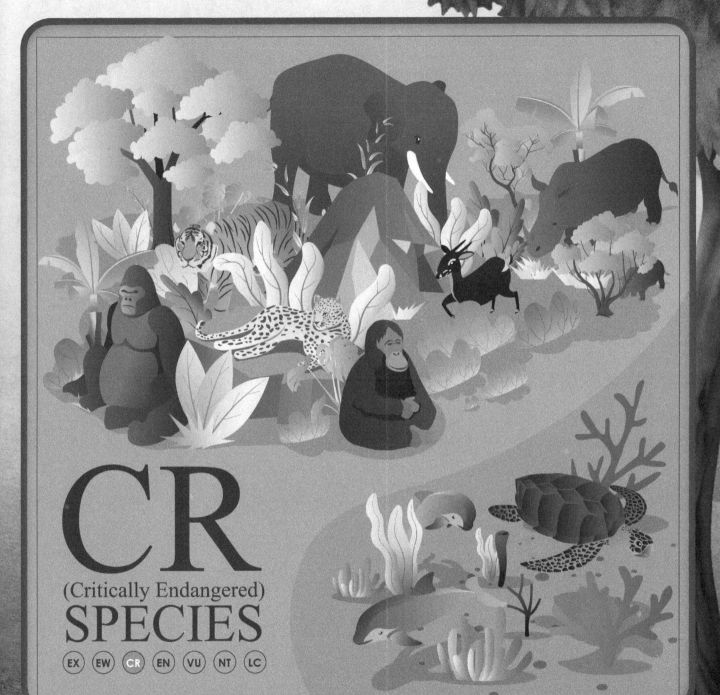

CR
(Critically Endangered)
SPECIES

EX EW CR EN VU NT LC

33

SUMATRAN RHINOS

The smallest species of rhinoceros, the Sumatran Rhino has two horns and long, woolly fur. Because of habitat loss, there are pockets of Sumatran Rhinos in the wild living in groups that are too small to sustain their numbers. The small groups cannot reach each other to breed and enhance the gene pool...at least not without human intervention. Currently, there are only about 80 Sumatran Rhinos left in the world. Scientists have tried breeding programs for the animals, but this has proven to be very difficult. Only two baby Sumatran Rhinos have been born in captivity in the last two decades.

Sumatran Rhinos

MOUNTAIN GORILLA

Native to the mountains of Uganda, Rwanda, and the Congo, the Mountain Gorillas are massive and powerful primates that can grow to weigh around 400 pounds. Their thick fur helps shield them from the cold mountain air. Primatologists believe there are just a little more than one thousand Mountain Gorillas still in existence. The population declined due to habitat destruction, poaching, and ongoing wars in their native lands. Many scientists, most notably Dian Fossey, helped to raise awareness for the plight of the Mountain Gorilla. Through diligent conservation efforts, the population of Mountain Gorillas is beginning to increase in recent years.

Mountain Gorilla

HAWKSBILL SEA TURTLES

There are only a few thousand Hawksbill Sea Turtles left in the oceans. For centuries, the beautiful turtle was hunted for its meat, eggs, and its distinctive shell. Today, this sea turtle is critically endangered. The loss of the Hawksbill Sea Turtle would cause a ripple effect across the coral reefs that the turtle calls home. It plays an important role in maintaining the balance of life and the health of coral reefs.

Hawksbill Sea Turtle

45

RED PANDAS

Red Pandas look more like raccoons than they do their cousins, the black and white Giant Pandas we are all familiar with. Red Pandas, native to the forests of the Himalayan Mountains, have reddish fur and are just a little bit bigger than an average house cat. Like the Giant Panda, the Red Pandas eat primarily a diet of bamboo. As the bamboo forests of the region are destroyed so is the habitat for the Red Pandas. There are only about 10,000 Red Pandas left and that number has been on a steady decline.

Red Panda

The most endangered animal in the world, the Vaquita, is probably an animal you've never heard of before. This smallest member of the porpoise family is found only in the Gulf of California. The Vaquita is identified by its oversized dorsal fin and the dark circles around its eyes. The Vaquitas are rather elusive so it is difficult for marine biologists to get exact numbers, but it is believed that that are less than 20 of this small and shy porpoise species remaining.

Vaquita

SUMATRAN TIGERS

Native to Sumatra, an island in Indonesia, the Sumatran Tiger is currently critically endangered. Only about 400 to 500 of the Sumatran Tigers, the smallest of the tiger species, are left, due to the loss of their habitat and poaching by hunters. The tigers live in small groups scattered across the national parks of Sumatra. There were once other tiger species in the Sunda Islands, including the Javan Tiger and the Bali Tiger, but they went extinct, leaving the Sumatran Tiger as the only tiger species remaining in Indonesia.

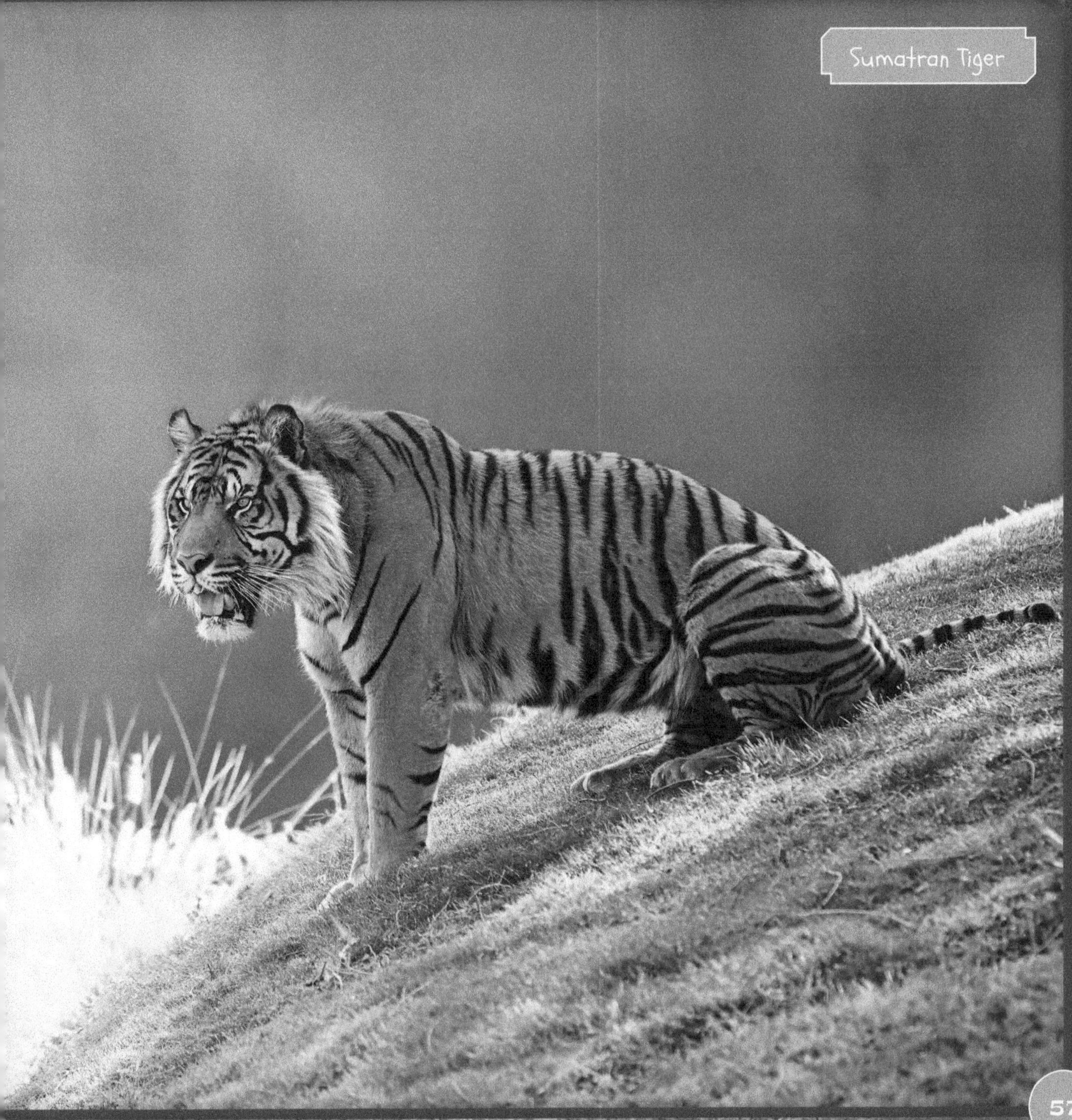
Sumatran Tiger

PANGOLINS

There are eight different varieties of Pangolin and all of them are endangered. The Pangolin may remind you of an armadillo. It is a nocturnal mammal that is covered with rows of thick scales. When confronted with a predator, the Pangolin will roll itself up into an impenetrable ball. Pangolins are targeted by illegal hunters who sell the animals for meat and for their scales. For the wealthy elite in some parts of Asia, Pangolin meat is a special and expensive treat. Folk tales claim that the Pangolin has medicinal properties, too, so it is often hunted for use as a folk remedy. Biologists believe that the Pangolin is the most poached animal in the world.

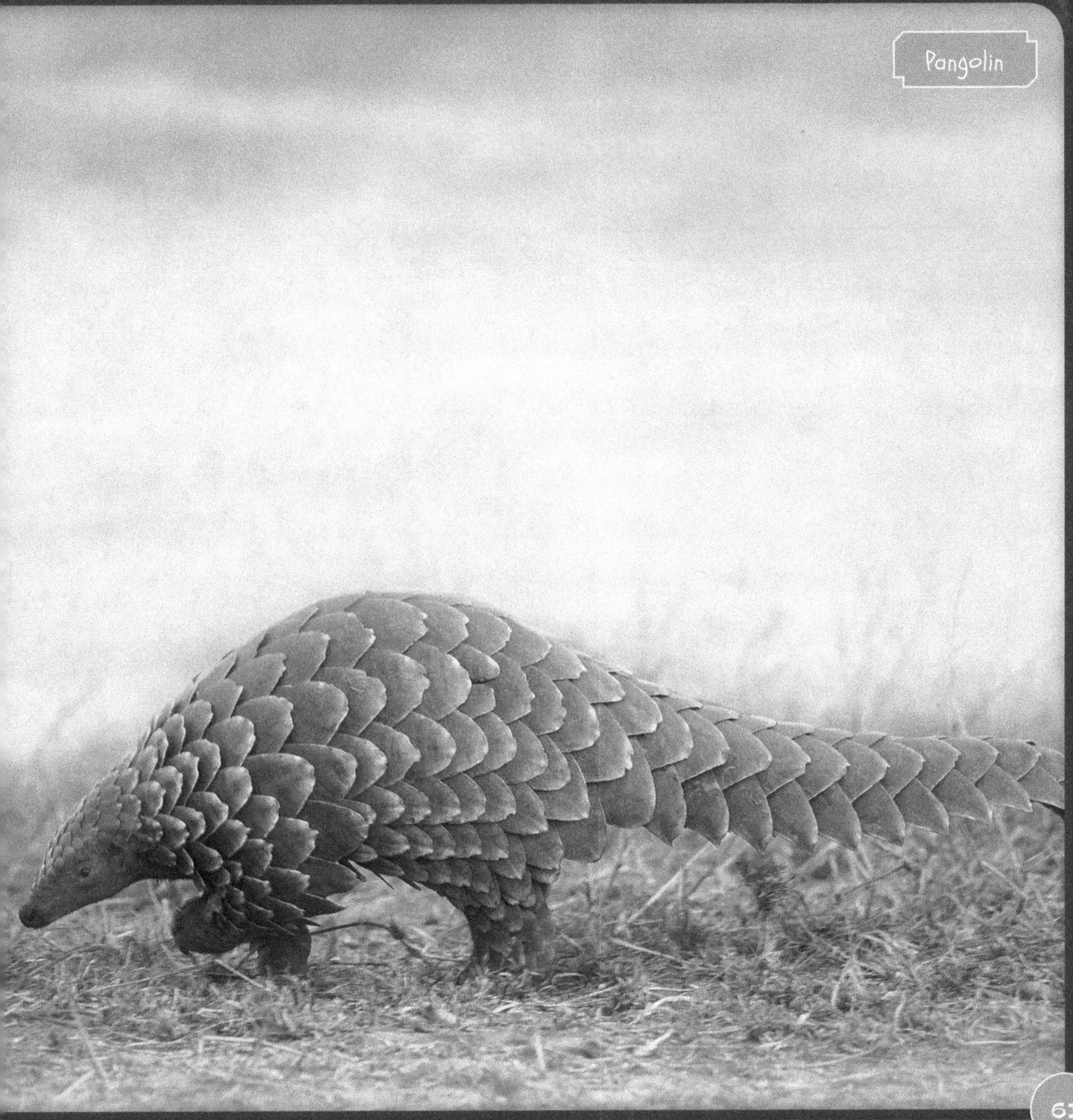
Pangolin

Second only to the Blue Whale in size, the Fin Whale is a very large variety of whale with a noticeable ridge along its back. Oddly, the whales have a white right jaw and a black left jaw that marine biologists believe help them to herd fish into tight schools to make them easier to eat. In the 1800s and 1900s, the Fin Whales were hunted to near extinction, but since 1973, they have been protected from whaling. They are still listed as endangered, though their numbers are increasing.

Fin Whale

AMUR LEOPARD

The Amur Leopard is native to the temperate forests of Russia. However, poaching, logging, and a diminishing food source pushed the Amur Leopard to the brink of extinction. Just ten years ago, biologists estimated that there were only about 30 of these fast and agile big cats left in the wild, but current conservation practices seem to be helping this species. Today, the population has doubled to around 60.

Amur Leopard

69

In the last twenty years, roughly 85% of the habitat of Orangutans has been lost due to agriculture and deforestation which has had devastating impacts on their population totals. Additionally, about a third of the Orangutan population was killed in wildfires in the late 1990s. Even as their numbers decline, poachers and illegal pet traders continue to take the animals. By some estimates, between two and three thousand Orangutans are killed by poachers each year. If the current trend continues, the Orangutans could go extinct by 2070.

Orangutan

73

WHAT CAN YOU DO TO HELP ENDANGERED ANIMALS?

When thinking about the plight of endangered animals, you may be moved to do something to help them. Fortunately, there are some steps that you can take to help. First, you can let other people know about endangered species, so they are also aware. You can do all you can to help protect the environment and reduce the need to use natural resources. You could also support the conservation efforts of others, either by volunteering for a conservation[6] organization or by donating money to help fund the work that they do. If you are passionate about animal conservation, you could even consider a future career as a biologist or animal conservationist.

[6] Conservation – The act of conserving, preventing loss or death

Support the conservation efforts of others by volunteering for a conservation organization.

There are many animals that are currently living on the planet that are close to going extinct like the dinosaurs did millions of years ago. Some extinctions are part of the natural progression of life on Earth, but too many of them are threatened due to the activities of humans. Animals are listed on the Red List of Threatened Species which ranks them based on population numbers and threats to their habitats. You can help protect endangered animals by raising awareness and supporting the efforts of animal conservationists.

Help protect endangered animals by raising awareness and supporting the efforts of animal conservationists.

Now that you understand how close some animals are to extinction, you are ready to learn more about ways that we can protect the environment to help both people and animals.

Visit

www.speedypublishing.com

To view and download free content on your favorite subject and browse our catalog of new and exciting books for readers of all ages.